Life is beautiful
for Clarinet Quartet

Score

GW00891043

Beguine ♩ = 145
Cheer up Giosuè

Lento ♩ = 60
The train in the dark

Life is beautiful
for Clarinet Quartet

N. Piovani

Cl.I

Life is beautiful
for Clarinet Quartet

Life is beautiful

for Clarinet Quartet

Cl.Bs.

N. Piovani

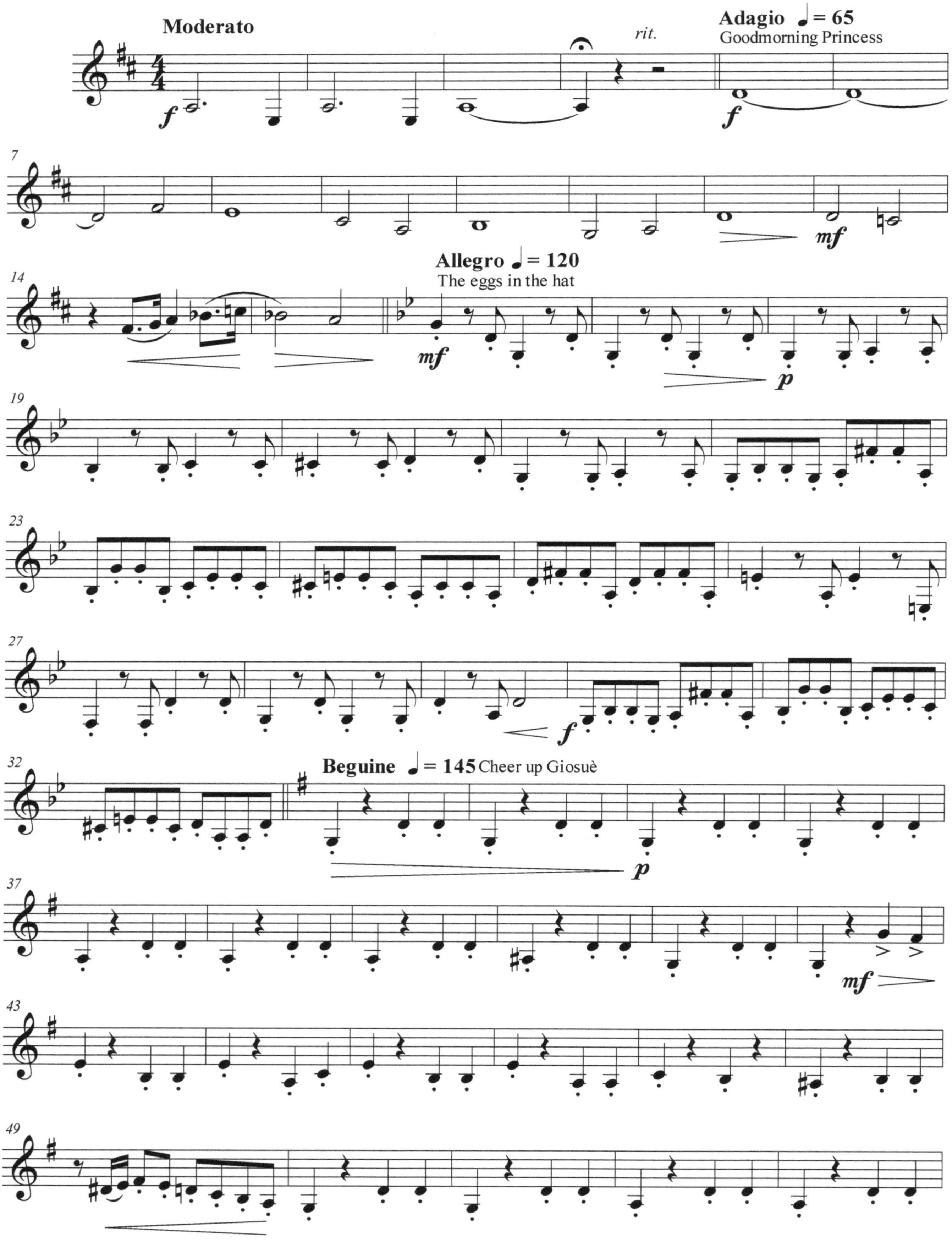